This book belongs to:

_____

_____

_____

D0579662

Days to Remember

A Keepsake Book for Birthdays, Anniversaries & Special Occasions

Written and Illustrated by

Donna Green

SMITHMARK

Copyright © 1995 Fremont & Green Ltd., Inc.
Illustrations copyright © 1995 Donna Green

All rights reserved. No part of this publication may be reproduced, stored in
a retrieval system or transmitted in any form by any means electronic,
mechanical, photocopying or otherwise, without first obtaining written
permission of the copyright owner.

This edition published in 1995 by SMITHMARK Publishers Inc.
16 East 32nd Street, New York, NY 10016

SMITHMARK books are available for bulk purchase for
sales promotions and premium use.
For details write or telephone the manager of special sales,
SMITHMARK Publishers, Inc., 16 East 32nd Street
New York, NY 10016; (212) 532-6600

Produced by VIA Rob Fremont, Inc.
c/o Vermilion
P.O. Box 144
Norwell, MA 02061

A Rob Fremont Book

Design by Berge Zerdelian
Editor: Oliver Fremont
Composition: Garbo Typesetting

ISBN: 0-8317-2176-6

Printed and bound in Singapore by Imago Publishing Ltd

10 9 8 7 6 5

List of Paintings

I love people. I love my family, my children . . . but inside myself is a place where I live all alone and that's where you renew your springs that never dry up.
                                                                        —PEARL S. BUCK

January

My grandmother's name was Sarah. She had six children, twenty-two grandchildren, and twenty great grandchildren. She was a quiet lady with a gentle smile, loving eyes and enough faith for the entire family. Every January she would start crocheting socks and mittens for all her grandchildren's Christmas gifts the following December. So when we opened our brightly colored packages we knew that she had been thinking of us the entire year. Now, when I'm bundling up my children in layers of clothing so they can play in the snow, my cherished mittens, now faded and full of holes, are the last garments to be put on over newer gloves. Grandma Green would have liked that.

January

1752 Betsy Ross

NEW YEAR'S DAY

1

2

1879 Grace Coolidge
1898 ZaSu Pitts
1905 Anna May Wong

3

1914 Jane Wyman
1937 Grace Bumbry

4

January

1946 Diane Keaton

5

1412 Joan of Arc

6

1903 Zora Neale Hurston

7

M*aking the decision to have a child – it's momentous. It is to decide forever to have your heart go walking around outside your body.*
— ELIZABETH STONE

January

1638 Elisabetta Sirani
1867 Emily Greene Balch

8

1908 Simone de Beauvoir
1854 Jennie Jerome Churchill
1941 Joan Baez

9

1903 Barbara Hepworth

10

1899 Eva Le Gallienne

11

January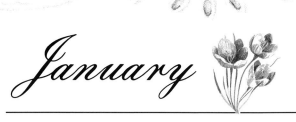

12

1884 Sophie Tucker

13

1942 Faye Dunaway

14

. . . As long as one keeps searching, the answers come.
— JOAN BAEZ

January

1937 Margaret O'Brien

15

1909 Ethel Merman

16

1820 Anne Brontë
1934 Shari Lewis

17

*M*id pleasures and palaces though we may roam
Be it ever so humble, there's no place like home.

–JOHN HOWARD PAYNE

January

18

1905 Oveta Culp Hobby
1921 Patricia Highsmith

19

1926 Patricia Neal

20

21

January

22

1933 Chita Rivera

23

1862 Edith Wharton
1925 Maria Tallchief

24

N*o matter how old a mother is she watches her middle-aged children for signs of improvement.*

—FLORIDA SCOTT MAXWELL

January

1882 Virginia Woolf

25

1831 Mary Dodge
1872 Julia Morgan
1928 Eartha Kitt

26

1921 Donna Reed

27

1933 Susan Sontag

28

January

1835 Sarah Chauncey Woolsey
1939 Germaine Greer

29

1912 Barbara Tuchman
1937 Vanessa Redgrave

30

1903 Tallulah Bankhead
1923 Carol Channing

31

There have been women in the past far more daring than we would need to be now, who ventured all and gained a little, but survived after all.

– GERMAINE GREER

I call February my 'nesting-in' month. It's when I keep the
wood stove stoked and paint cozy scenes of children playing
by the hearth. There are a lot of good things about February. It's
a wonderful time to get reacquainted with your children; to sew;
to renew old friendships over the telephone; to organize things;
to write letters; to plan your spring garden; to dream.

February

1921 Betty Hutton

26

1888 Lotte Lehmann
1932 Elizabeth Taylor

27

28

1736 Ann Lee

29

March

This is the month which has always seemed magical to me. Signs of spring begin to appear giving rise to great expectations of warmer days. As children we would wait for the pussy willow branches to bloom and then make tiny rabbits from their fuzzy buds. I especially recall dressing up in pretty clothes and organizing tea parties for our cat, Tabby, who always seemed to have other plans.

*G*od sent children . . . to enlarge our hearts and to make us unselfish . . . to give our souls higher aims . . . and to bring round our firesides bright faces, happy smiles and loving, tender hearts.

—MARY BOTHAM HOWITT

March

1

1919 Jennifer Jones
1950 Karen Carpenter

2

1911 Jean Harlow

3

1939 Paula Prentiss

4

March

1946 Liza Minelli

12

13

1836 Isabella Mary Beeton
1923 Diane Arbus

14

The events of childhood do not pass, but repeat themselves like seasons of the year.

— ELEANOR FARJEON

March

1933 Ruth Bader Ginsburg

15

1822 Rosa Bonheur

16

1846 Kate Greenaway
1873 Margaret Bondfield

17

We need time to dream, time to remember,
and time to reach the infinite. Time to be.

– GLADYS TABER

March

1865 Anna Held

18

1907 Elizabeth Maconchy
1947 Glenn Close

19

1917 Vera Lynn

20

1905 Phyllis McGinley

21

March

22

1857 Fannie Farmer
1908 Joan Crawford

23

24

In the sheltered simplicity of the first days after a baby is born, one sees again the magical closed circle. The miraculous sense of two people existing only for each other.

– ANNE MORROW LINDBERGH

March

1925 Flannery O'Connor
1934 Gloria Steinem
1942 Aretha Franklin

25

1930 Sandra Day O'Connor
1944 Diana Ross

26

1899 Gloria Swanson

27

1922 Grace Hartigan
1952 Donna Green

28

March

29

1820 Anna Sewell

30

1929 Liz Claiborne
1934 Shirley Jones
1936 Marge Piercy

31

The passage is through, not over, not by, not around but through.
— CHERRIE MORAGA

April

Each spring my mother makes her way into the back field and picks sweet smelling branches of apple blossoms. Not too many. Just enough to fill her kitchen with a reminder that another cold winter has come and gone. Her ways are quiet and simple, yet the little things she has always done, like gathering berries to bake a pie or going over my homework when I was a child, are as special to me as all the riches in the world.

*A*rranging a bowl of flowers in the morning can give a sense of quiet in a crowded day — like writing a poem, or saying a prayer.

— ANNE MORROW LINDBERGH

April

1932 Debbie Reynolds

1

2

1924 Doris Day

3

1802 Dorothea Dix
1928 Maya Angelou

4

April

1908 Bette Davis

5

1944 Michelle Phillips

6

1893 Irene Castle
1915 Billie Holiday

7

Never grow a wishbone, daughter, where your backbone ought to be.
— CLEMENTINE PADDLEFORD

April

1893 Mary Pickford
1912 Sonja Henie
1918 Betty Ford

8

1827 Maria Susanna Cummins
1888 Florence Price

9

1880 Frances Perkins
1903 Clare Boothe Luce

10

1865 Mary White Ovington
1928 Ethel Kennedy
1941 Ellen Goodman

11

April

1883 Imogen Cunningham
1904 Lily Pons

12

1909 Eudora Welty

13

1941 Julie Christie

14

If you have made mistakes . . . there is always another chance for you . . . you may have a fresh start any moment you choose, for this thing we call "failure" is not the falling down, but the staying down.

— MARY PICKFORD

April

1898 Bessie Smith
1933 Elizabeth Montgomery

15

1755 Elisabeth Vigée-Le Brun

16

1916 Sirimavo Bandaranaike

17

18

April

19

1949 Jessica Lange

20

1816 Charlotte Brontë

21

April

1766 Madame de Staël

22

1928 Shirley Temple Black

23

1931 Bridget Riley
1934 Shirley MacLaine
1942 Barbra Streisand

24

1900 Edith Halpert
1918 Ella Fitzgerald

25

April

26
1893 Anita Loos
1895 Dorothea Lange
1934 Carol Burnett

27
1759 Mary Wollstonecraft Godwin

28
1941 Ann Margaret

29
1917 Maya Deren
1957 Michelle Pfeiffer

30
1912 Eve Arden

May

When my daughter was a toddler she liked to help me weed my garden. I always told her what a good job she was doing even though most of her weeds had flowers on top. When she was three she would chew on chives or show me how lemon balm made her hands smell sweet. But that was long ago. The other day she served me a cup of soothing chamomile tea made from herbs which she grew in her own garden. I have always loved my gardens, now more than ever, because that is where my daughter and I became friends.

My favourite thing is to go where I've never been.

– DIANE ARBUS

May

1852 Martha "Calamity Jane" Burk
1909 Kate Smith
1945 Rita Coolidge

1

1895 Peggy Bacon

2

1912 May Sarton

3

1929 Audrey Hepburn

4

May

1867 Nellie Bly

5

6

1868 Gail Laughlin

7

Backward, turn backward, O time in your flight,
Make me a child again just for tonight!
Mother, come back from the echoless shore,
Take me again to your heart as of yore.

— ELIZABETH AKERS ALLEN

May

8

1936 Glenda Jackson
1946 Candice Bergen

9

1919 Ella Grasso

10

1884 Alma Gluck
1893 Martha Graham

11

May

1820 Florence Nightingale
1883 Hazel Harrison

12

1907 Daphne du Maurier

13

14

There is a point where you aren't as much mom and daughter as you are adults and friends.

–JAMIE LEE CURTIS

May

1857 Williamina Fleming
1890 Katherine Anne Porter

15

16

17

A mother is a person who seeing there are only four pieces of pie for five people, promptly announces she never did care for pie.

– TENNEVA JORDAN

May

18

1930 Lorraine Hansberry
1941 Nora Ephron

19

1768 Dolly Madison
1946 Cher

20

1780 Elizabeth Fry

21

May

1844 Mary Cassatt

22

1810 Margaret Fuller
1889 Mabel Walker Willebrandt
1933 Joan Collins

23

1883 Elsa Maxwell
1934 Jane Margaret Byrne

24

God could not be everywhere, and therefore he made mothers.

— JEWISH PROVERB

May

1929 Beverly Sills
1943 Leslie Uggams

25

1966 Helena Bonham-Carter

26

1819 Julia Ward Howe
1878 Isadora Duncan

27

28

May

29

30

1824 Jessie Benton Fremont

31

During the first weeks, I used to lie long hours with the baby in my arms, watching her asleep; sometimes catching a gaze from her eyes: feeling very near the edge, the mystery, perhaps the knowledge of life.

– ISADORA DUNCAN

June

I too was a June bride once upon a time – or as my Adam would say, back in the good old days. The old days, in my case, was the time when flower children bloomed. I planned my reception to take place in a serenely beautiful field overlooking a river. The day was perfect with friends and family having a wonderful time singing and dancing and contracting poison ivy. Everyone still remembers *my* wedding!

. . . *And suddenly I realized that it would all happen. I would be his wife, we would walk in the garden together, we would stroll down that path in the valley to the shingle beach. I knew how I would stand on the steps after breakfast, looking at the day, throwing crumbs to the birds, and later wander out in a shady hat with long scissors in my hand, and cut flowers for the house.*

– DAPHNE du MAURIER

June

1926 Marilyn Monroe

1

1731 Martha Washington

2

1906 Josephine Baker

3

1852 Mary Kingsley

4

June

1939 Margaret Drabble
1942 Tammy Wynette

5

1898 Ninette de Valois

6

1909 Jessica Tandy
1917 Gwendolyn Brooks

7

You will do foolish things, but do them with enthusiasm.

– COLETTE

June

1925 Barbara Bush

8

9

1895 Hattie McDaniel
1922 Judy Garland

10

1815 Julia Margaret Cameron
1880 Jeannette Rankin

11

June

1929 Anne Frank

12

1875 Miriam Amanda Ferguson
1908 Marie Vieira da Silva

13

1811 Harriet Beecher Stowe
1906 Margaret Bourke-White

14

When you get into a tight place and everything goes against you, till it seems as though you could not hang on a minute longer, never give up then, for that is just the place and time that the tide will turn.

–HARRIET BEECHER STOWE

June

15

1917 Katharine Graham
1938 Joyce Carol Oates

16

17

1903 Jeanette MacDonald
1913 Sylvia Porter
1937 Gail Godwin

18

June

1887 Blanche Yurka
1954 Kathleen Turner

19

1905 Lillian Hellman
1947 Anne Murray

20

1912 Mary McCarthy
1925 Maureen Stapleton

21

In the effort to give good and comforting answers to the young questioners whom we love, we very often arrive at good and comforting answers for ourselves. —RUTH GOODE

June

1906 Anne Morrow Lindbergh
1949 Meryl Streep

22

1929 June Carter
1940 Wilma Rudolph

23

24

1945 Carly Simon

25

June

---

1892 Pearl S. Buck
1914 Laurie Lee
1914 Mildred Didrikson Zaharias

26

1869 Emma Goldman
1880 Helen Keller

27

1891 Esther Forbes

28

29

1918 Lena Horne

30

I have come back again to where I belong; not an enchanted place,
but the walls are strong.   – DOROTHY H. RATH

July

A firecracker pops, a volley ball game begins and another fully dressed, squealing woman is thrown into the lake. It's the annual Fourth of July family reunion at Aunt Ida's and Uncle Mike's. For the umpteenth year in a row, my dad's fried clams are the treat of the day. And, of course, there is never a quiet moment once Aunt Jenny arrives with a serious gleam in her eye and a drop of salt on her tongue. Doesn't every family have its own personal mischief maker? My family truly knows how to have fun. If only I could bottle our summer get togethers for occasional sips all year long.

July

1916 Olivia De Havilland
1941 Twyla Tharp

1

2

3

1876 Sophie Irene Loeb
1898 Gertrude Lawrence
1918 Abigail van Buren/Ann Landers

INDEPENDENCE DAY, 1776

4

July

5

1917 Dorothy Kirsten
1923 Nancy Reagan

6

7

It had long since come to my attention that *people of accomplishment rarely sat back and let things happen to them. They went out and happened to things.*

—ELINOR SMITH

July

1867 Käthe Kollwitz

8

1764 Ann Radcliffe
1893 Dorothy Thompson

9

1830 Camille Pissarro
1875 Mary McLeod Bethune
1923 Jean Kerr

10

1854 Georgiana Drew Barrymore

11

July

1971 Kristi Yamaguchi

12

13

1930 Polly Bergen

14

Everyone has a talent. What is rare is the courage to follow
the talent to the dark places where it leads.

– ERICA JONG

July

1850 Frances Xavier Cabrini

15

1821 Mary Baker Eddy
1906 Barbara Stanwyck
1911 Ginger Rogers

16

1796 Camille Corot
1917 Phyllis Diller

17

*M*ake a memory with your children,
Spend some time to show you care;
Toys and trinkets can't replace those
Precious moments that you share.

– ELAINE HARDT

July

1852 Gertrude Käsebier

18

19

1885 Theda Bara
1938 Natalie Wood

20

1856 Louise Blanchard Bethune
1938 Janet Reno

21

July

29

30

1894 Blanche Knopf
1940 Patricia Schroeder

31

If you bungle raising your children, I don't think whatever
else you do well matters very much.

– JACQUELINE KENNEDY ONASSIS

One is not born a woman – one becomes one.

– SIMONE DE BEAUVOIR

August

Then one day you floated down the stairs in crinoline
and lace, a butterfly at last. What happened to gangly legs,
picture books and climbing trees?

August

1764 Anne Willing Bingham
1878 Eva Tanguay
1881 Edna Sewell

1

1900 Helen Morgan

2

1920 P. D. James

3

4

August

5

1881 Louella Parsons
1905 Clara Bow
1911 Lucille Ball

6

1876 Margaretha Zelle

7

The best advice from my mother was a reminder to tell my children everyday: "Remember you are loved."

– EVELYN McCORMICK

August

1884 Sara Teasdale
1896 Marjorie Kinnan Rawlings
1923 Esther Williams

8

9

10

1823 Charlotte Mary Yonge
1897 Enid Blyton

11

August

12

1860 Annie Oakley

13

1926 Alice Adams

14

The ability to laugh at life is right at the top, with love and communication, in the hierarchy of our needs.

— SARA DAVIDSON

One can never consent to creep when one feels an impulse to soar.
– HELEN KELLER

August

1879 Ethel Barrymore
1887 Edna Ferber
1912 Julia Child

15

1931 Eydie Gorme
1945 Suzanne Farrell

16

1892 Mae West

17

Living the past is a dull and lonely business; looking back strains the neck muscles, causes you to bump into people not going your way.

– EDNA FERBER

August

1587 Virginia Dare

18

1885 Grace Hutchins
1940 Jill St John

19

1818 Emily Brontë
1946 Connie Chung

20

21

August

1893 Dorothy Parker

22

23

1965 Marlee Matlin

24

The best way to keep children home is to make the home atmosphere pleasant – and let the air out of the tires.

–DOROTHY PARKER

August

1927 Althea Gibson

25

1935 Geraldine Ferraro

26

1916 Martha Raye

27

1774 Elizabeth Ann Bayley Seton

28

August

1916 Ingrid Bergman

29

1797 Mary Shelley
1909 Virginia Lee Burton

30

1870 Maria Montessori

31

You can aim for what you want and if you don't get it, you don't get it, but if you don't aim you don't get anything.

— FRANCINE PROSE

September

Every fall, it's a tradition in my family to go apple picking at Walling Ford's Farm with our Aunty Ruth from Maine. One day in particular stands out like a shiny penny in my trunk of rich memories of my son, Adam. He was so grown up that day, my little man of five, strutting through the orchard with the grand purpose of finding the most perfect apple. Why should I have been surprised that this apple would be perched on top of one of the tallest trees around. He climbed up that tree like a knight after his dragon, with me wincing every time he broke a twig. As he poked his head through the top of the tree he gave his Dad the biggest grin, and triumphantly held the apple up over his head. "I did it" he exclaimed. I think that was the sweetest apple he ever gave me.

If you obey all the rules you miss all the fun.

– KATHARINE HEPBURN

September

1898 Marilyn Miller
1924 Yvonne Decarlo
1939 Lily Tomlin

1

1820 Lucretia Hale

2

1849 Sarah Orne Jewett
1915 Kitty Carlisle
1933 Ann Richards

3

1931 Mitzi Gaynor

4

September

1940 Raquel Welch

5

1860 Jane Addams
1947 Jane Curtin

6

1860 Grandma Moses
1900 Taylor Caldwell
1947 Ann Beattie

7

September

1863 Jessie Willcox Smith

8

1868 Mary Austin

9

10

1943 Lola Falana

11

September

12

1903 Claudette Colbert
1946 Jaqueline Bisset

13

1879 Margaret Sanger
1897 Margaret Rudkin
1934 Kate Millet

14

The time when you need to do something is when no one else is willing to do it, when people are saying it can't be done.

— MARY FRANCES BERRY

September

1890 Agatha Christie

15

1924 Lauren Bacall

16

1931 Anne Bancroft
1934 Maureen Connolly

17

1905 Greta Garbo

18

September

1943 Cass Elliott
1949 Twiggy
1950 Joan Lunden

19

1928 Joyce Brothers
1934 Sophia Loren

20

21

Who ran to help me when I fell
And would some pretty story tell,
Or kiss the place to make it well?
My mother.

– ANN TAYLOR

September

1830 Caroline Webster Schermerhorn Astor
1956 Debby Boone

22

1900 Louise Nevelson

23

24

1931 Barbara Walters

25

September

26

27

1856 Kate Wiggin
1881 Eleanora Sears

28

1810 Elizabeth Cleghorn Gaskell

29

30

October

I have always felt that picking out the right pumpkin for our family Halloween jack-o-lantern is a ritual similar to buying a car. Every member of the family holds a strong opinion. We can spend an incredible amount of time going back and forth between my son, who thinks the best pumpkins must be on the bottom of the huge pile, and my daughter, who thinks we should select one that is as big as she. I always like the small round ones and my husband likes the large oval ones. Common sense usually prevails and we buy four pumpkins.

You may be disappointed if you fail, but you are doomed if you don't try.

– BEVERLY SILLS

October

1893 Faith Baldwin
1931 Angie Dickinson
1935 Julie Andrews

1

2

1899 Gertrude Berg

3

4

October

5

1908 Carole Lombard

6

1907 Helen MacInnes
1923 June Allyson

7

October

1949 Sigourney Weaver

8

1890 Aimee Semple McPherson

9

1900 Helen Hayes
1958 Tanya Tucker

10

1884 Eleanor Roosevelt

11

October

1889 Perle Mesta

12

1853 Lillie Langtry
1925 Margaret Thatcher

13

1896 Lillian Gish
1906 Hannah Arendt
1941 Anne Rice

14

Nobody can make you feel inferior without your consent.

– ELEANOR ROOSEVELT

October

1906 Alicia Patterson
1943 Penny Marshall

15

1925 Angela Lansbury

16

1918 Rita Hayworth

17

*T*o every thing there is a season, and a time to every purpose under the heaven; A time to be born, and a time to die; a time to plant, and a time to pluck up that which is planted. – ECCLESIASTES 3:1,2

October

1889 Fannie Hurst
1956 Martina Navratilova

18

19

1904 Anna Neagle

20

1929 Ursula LeGuin

21

October

1845 Sarah Bernhardt
1943 Catherine Deneuve

22

23

1923 Denise Levertov

24

My mother gave me to the moons,
And gave in turn the moons to me,
One midnight when she sang her tunes
To a baby on her knee.

—HANIEL LONG

October

1941 Helen Reddy
1941 Anne Tyler

25

1911 Mahalia Jackson
1947 Hillary Rodham Clinton

26

1872 Emily Post
1923 Ruby Dee
1932 Sylvia Plath

27

1939 Jane Alexander

28

October

1891 Fannie Brice

29

1896 Ruth Gordon

30

1950 Jane Pauley   HALLOWEEN

31

When you look at your life, the greatest happinesses are family happinesses.
– JOYCE BROTHERS

November

I love Thanksgiving! I could spend the entire month of
November day dreaming about Aunt Ruth's cinnamon rolls
or grandma's heavenly pie. Its the one time of year I allow myself
my own mincemeat squares. Sometimes I think we should write
a family cookbook because every far flung member seems to be
hoarding the secret recipe for some dish fit for royalty. Most of all, I
love Thanksgiving because it brings so many of us together at one time.

November

1

1755 Marie Antoinette
1892 Alice Brady

2

3

4

November

1857 Ida Tarbell
1913 Vivian Leigh

5

1946 Sally Field

6

1943 Joni Mitchell

7

It is never too late to be what you might have been.

– GEORGE ELIOT

November

1900 Margaret Mitchell
1909 Katharine Hepburn

8

1869 Marie Dressler
1915 Hedy Lamarr
1928 Anne Sexton

9

10

1744 Abigail Adams
1872 Maude Adams

11

November

1751 Margaret Corbin
1815 Elizabeth Cady Stanton
1929 Grace Kelly

12

13

14

Age *does not protect you from love. But love, to some extent, protects you from age.*
— JEANNE MOREAU

November

1887 Marianne Moore
1887 Georgia O'Keeffe

15

1899 Mary Margaret McBride

16

17

1888 Frances Marion
1939 Brenda Vaccaro

18

November

1917 Indira Gandhi
1926 Jeane Kirkpatrick
1962 Jodie Foster

19

20

1902 Phoebe Omlie
1945 Goldie Hawn

21

What do girls do who haven't any mothers to help them through their troubles?

—LOUISA MAY ALCOTT

November

1819 George Eliot
1943 Billie Jean King
1958 Jamie Lee Curtis

22

23

1849 Frances Hodgson Burnett

24

1846 Carry Nation
1940 Tina Turner

25

November

26

1937 Gail Sheehy

27

1904 Nancy Mitford

28

1832 Louisa May Alcott
1918 Madeleine L'Engle

29

1924 Shirley Chisholm

30

No pessimist ever discovered the secrets of the stars, or sailed to an uncharted land, or opened a new heaven to the human spirit.

−HELEN KELLER

December

*C*hestnuts sizzle over the hearth while spicy mulled cider is served to guests dropping by. The whole house is filled with the glorious scent of hemlock as little ones tug on branches trying to rehang garlands of strung popcorn and cranberries. And all the while, songs of Christmas float in the air like angels whispering prayers for a gentler world.

December

1913 Mary Martin
1945 Bette Midler

1

1884 Ruth Draper

2

1923 Maria Callas

3

1861 Lillian Russell

4

December

1830 Christina Rossetti
1934 Joan Didion

5

1906 Agnes Moorehead

6

1873 Willa Cather

7

Until you make peace with who you are, you'll never be content with what you have.

– DORIS MORTMAN

December

8

9

1830 Emily Dickinson

10

1944 Brenda Lee

11

December

1928 Helen Frankenthaler
1931 Rita Moreno
1941 Dionne Warwick

12

1818 Mary Todd Lincoln

13

1897 Margaret Chase Smith
1935 Lee Remick
1946 Patty Duke

14

What feeling is so nice as a child's hand in yours? So small, so soft and warm, like a kitten huddling in the shelter of your clasp.

— MARJORIE HOLMES

December

1913 Muriel Rukeyser

15

1775 Jane Austen
1901 Margaret Mead

16

17

1916 Betty Grable

18

December

___

1865 Minnie Maddern Fiske

19

___

1886 Hazel Hotchkiss White
1904 Irene Dunn

20

___

1872 Helen Farnsworth Mears
1937 Jane Fonda

21

One of the oldest human needs is having someone to wonder where you
are when you don't come home at night.

– MARGARET MEAD

December

1912 Lady Bird Johnson
1945 Diane Sawyer

22

23

1922 Ava Gardner

24

1821 Clara Barton
1865 Fay Templeton

CHRISTMAS

25

December

26

1901 Marlene Dietrich

27

1934 Maggie Smith

28

Family faces are magic mirrors. Looking at people who belong to us, we
see the past, present and future.

– GAIL LUMET BUCKLEY

December

1721 Madame de Pompadour
1937 Mary Tyler Moore

29

30

1878 Elizabeth Arden
1927 Nancy Hanks
1948 Donna Summer

NEW YEAR'S EVE

31